Buffalo Five

Buffalo Five

POEMS

Rasunah Katz

Acknowledgments

My appreciation to editors of the following magazines where some of these poems first appeared, perhaps in an earlier version or under the penname Kiva:
Another Chicago Magazine, *Big River News Literary Issue*, *Coast Peddler*, *Mendocino Arts & Entertainment Magazine*, *San Francisco Poetry Flash*, *Ridge Review*, *Ten Mile River Press*, *Upriver/Downriver.* Poems have also appeared in the *Dan River Anthology* (1986), *Faces & Tongues Poetry & Prose* (Laughing Waters Press, 1986), *Dalmo'ma Anthology*, *The Mendocino Review* (1985), *The Napa Review* (1983,1984), *The Western Edge: 33 Poets* (Ten Mile River Press), *Caulooga Collage* #10, *Coyote Journal* #10, *Subud International Anthology*, and *New Settler.*

A special thank you to Karen Lewis for her expert guidance in getting the book into a printed format as well as her help in editing and design. I would like to thank Sharon Doubiago and Devreaux Baker for their encouragement and support over many years of sharing the written and spoken word.

ISBN # 978-0-9669620-3-1
Pelican Press
Albion, California

Cover art by Eva Katz
Line drawings by Sam Katz
"Old Woman" painting by Carmen Searles, Age 12

for Sam

Contents

"Memory is good for one astonishing thing it does:
it brings dreams back."

~Antonio Machado, *Selected Poems and Prose*

Poet's Notes

The title comes from a dream I had on October 15, 1979. In the dream I went to visit someone in my childhood neighborhood of Pondosa, in Northern California. There was an old gardener there who took me to his quarters–a small room with an old fashioned radio like the one I remember. It was large, shaped with a round top and a wire netting on the front. He gave me a book and told me to read a poem–his. When he handed me the book, I noticed it was wrapped in old newsprint. It was a small, red book. The book was called *Buffalo Five* and the poem had five lines. As I began to wake up, I struggled to remember them because they were, I thought, remarkable. I thought I had recalled the last two lines writing them down; but later I could not find them anywhere. The last lines were a key of some sort. I woke feeling lost, like something important was missing.

I associate this dream with another at about the same time. In the dream, my mother was recalling my birth. She said I arrived at home on a bright day in a small house in the valley. In the dream, I was trying to remember it when my eyes began to flutter with a bright golden light. It felt like powder snow falling through closed eyelids; and then I began to sing in a lonely voice. I remember thinking: this is the first wind of a newborn.

I have been listening for that sound, looking for those words, that book, those colors, in and out of dreams, poems and journals. Many of the earlier poems seem to come from a voice that the world has stopped listening to; it remains a lonely voice. These dreams remind me of the way crows drop to the field one by one, until a gathering has taken place and then one is left wondering what comes next.

Rasunah Katz
Spring 2012

Bear Creek

My sister and I walked
two miles,
down the railroad tracks,
chasing lizards
in and out of the ties.
Cattle grazed on the hills
slow and lazy.
We swam down into that
ice water   snow water.
Swam against the rapids.
The excitement of getting
to the top,
so much work,
going to the bottom,
then surfacing.
The whole world, a single light,
shimmering through the alders.
Swim out to the sandbar,
you can make it.
I went down for the third time,
then came up to see
three or four big guys,
friends of hers
diving in.
We were children of the sun,

the afternoons
blackened our skin.
Pulled to the earth
we set our rhythms there,
breathing and resting,
the same as the wind
that came up strong
around 4 o'clock.
There was time then
to watch the water spiders
skipping across the stilled creek
to listen to the far off train whistle,
which would come
barreling over the trestle,
a signal of the late hour,
the long, hot and dusty walk home.

~ She'll tear a whole in you ~ Lumineers
but I love her anyway

The Hunt

My father and I
set out to hunt,
driving the pickup
over a log.
When it would go
no further,
we went on foot.
He carried a gun,
I walked silent in the meadow.
He seemed to lose
scent of the deer.
He bent to show me
a snake,
in the glint
of sunlight,
an extension
of the brown-yellow
long grass.
The smell of the forest
was damp ferns.
We walked miles,
listened intently
for a sign of the buck.
My father walked ahead.
I waited,

silent in the meadow.
He came back,
said the sun was too high.
From the look in his eye,
I knew he had been hunting,
hunting old memories,
hunting the trails
of his people,
hunting his ancestors,
the deer.

This is Pondosa

This is Pondosa.
A small logging camp
in Northern California.
To reach it you drive
two miles off Highway 89
on a dirt road.
In the winter
the road is impassable.
The train arrives
every two weeks
with supplies.
In the summer
the dust on that road
is two feet deep.
This is the house
my father lives in.
He's a train hostler.
He walks to work
with a bottle of Jim Beam
in his back pocket.
This is the rock garden.
Cinder rock.
Lava rock.
Obsidian.
This is Burney Falls.
Mt. Shasta to the East.

Bear Creek to the South.
Fall River Mills.
This is Medicine Lake.
I once cupped water
in my hands.
Evening came
for the first time.
She was barefoot
& slipped into the lake
turning over & over.
I watched her
spread herself there
until I could
no longer see her.
Then I slipped in myself
treading water
trying to spin her to me.
These are the woods.
Ponderosa Pine.
Douglas Fir.
Cedar.
Manzanita.
Dogwood.
It is sometimes still,
sometimes dark.

Around here
the lakes are like glass.
On the shore
her figure rides out,
always alone.
Once we dove down together
mute beyond the rocks
& lay there,
until bursting for air
we came up,
poppies.

Wings I

He had a shot glass hidden
in the lower left hand cabinet.
Up early, I'd hear him in the kitchen,
a couple of shots he'd be off,
trudging through the snow
to the round table.
That's where they kept the engines,
they had all these changing tracks.
Sometimes he took me with him,
lifted me high into the seat of the locomotive
then fire it up, the roar so deafening,
I'd cling to him, he'd laugh,
touch my hair softly,
like wings.
I went with him half out of fear,
half because I loved his big body,
the way I fit into it.

Wings II

Once when I was eight or nine, on a darkened day
just before the rain, they came out. They were called
flying rain beetles. They were large and black.
We chased them with sticks, relentlessly felled them,
smashed them to the ground; until the ground too,
was dark with them. Now just before each storm,
I look out, think about why we killed them like that.
I think about what darkness means, the sound of those
solid bodies hitting the board.

McCloud

The movie theater had two tiers. No, it was one tier
and then a half tier, maybe 30 seats in it.
One night, when his girlfriend worked late,
he waited for her in the half tier, in the back.
They didn't talk, they watched the movie.
It was about the war and this woman called High Pockets.
She hid top secrets inside her blouse.
Maybe it was the anticipation of what would happen
if they caught her or the way his little finger
caressed her hand, softly like wings.
Now she only likes it like that, when it's secret,
when she hardly knows it's happening
and when it's so soft
it feels like butterflies landing
all over her body.

Chileo Was Not the First

My mother reclined in her bedroom with a newspaper
spread around her. Time was running out.
My father was the rock, without him I had no ally.
I spent my days dreaming of the only Indian boyfriend
I ever had. His girlfriend told me
he started up with her when she was twelve.
He came to see me after my father died.
The TV was on.
He couldn't understand why it was taking so long
to get in. He had heard some stories about me and
Chileo Rodriquez, but they weren't true. Just some
boy's dream: *I think I just gave you what you really want.*
No, it's you I want, I whispered.
It's you, I want you so much.
Time was running out. The smell of his leather jacket
like some wild musk root, like the smell that leads you
into the damp forest. When I asked my mother about
sex, she said:
You just let a man go where he has to go, that's all.
I never believed her. The sounds she made in bed
with my father belied something else,
something wild like the cry of coyotes.
I left home the next day. I was sixteen. My mother said:
I gave birth to you, that's all.
Time was running out.
My father was the rock.

The Opening

I hardly understood it
even then,
why we were doing it,
or wanting to do it.
There was something
urgent about it
always my mother
in the next room,
feigning reading
or watching television.
I always knew,
I think he did too,
that she was there,
maybe even listening.
A silent condoning
of the act.
All that rubbing
against each other,
all that moaning,
was only,
leading up to it.
The electric moment,
of entering,
being inside,
enclosing one another.

꧁ 25 ꧂

Just a few sharp moments,
then years of remembering,
years of telling,
retelling
the loss.
What is it?
The first letting in.
And then opening,
that's it, isn't it?
It's the opening so deep
that all the ancestors enter
then you're tied forever
even years later
like a quickening
you feel it,
like someone
whispering
inside you.

The Opening II

Her life has had many openings
The first was entering this world
The second was her first love
He was an Indian boy, she was a girl of 15
No matter how long she tries to remember the first
It evaporates like a steam, all misty and unclear
The second lives in her body, never forgets
It is a whisper whenever love comes near
Like a gentle stream, it accompanies her
It never abandons, it lives side by side
Like some holy blessing
Like one who notices for the first time
The impeccable whiteness of snow
The third is something indescribable
With a language all its own
It finds the song in her
Soft as a lullaby she hears in memory
It grows into a cacophony of sounds and movements
Until she is no longer here   but there
Where the opening is so large without edges
or boundaries
What's left is emptiness
The one feeling that unites all the openings
Even the one that waits for us.

The Opening III

She lingers in that memory
As though it were yesterday
As though she were looking into a mirror
Reading the lines of her body
Touched so long ago.

You might ask why after all these years it comes to her
Sometimes in a lush & motionless moment
Sometimes like a thundering of hooves in the heart
It begins as an ember   the color of amber
Or when the day is ordinary & dreamless.

Sometimes she hears the name-calling
Something incomplete left undone
She sees the long brown arms of her youth
Reaching up for that immensity for that current
That unending river of damp earth,

That fierce innocent opening
Into a turquoise sky.

Chico I

He said, *Cold tonight. Must be real cold in Chico.*
Chico. Growing up in the fifties.
You had a few choices. You could go to Chico State
become a teacher or get married and have kids,
let your husband work at the mill.
Every noon hour the whistle would blow so long
and so loud, you could get lonely
hearing a sound like that. I passed through Chico
one night when I was fifteen. The sound outside
my boyfriend's window was even lonelier
than the mill whistle.
They were hollow,
mostly human sounds
but they didn't settle natural, not anywhere.
The next morning I left by bus. Never went back.
Later, he asked me why I wasn't pregnant.
He was ready for that. *Just blind luck.*
I read in a newspaper he graduated from Chico,
married a dental assistant.

Chico II

Chico can be a cold place. If you go on up
towards Red Bluff, head off east straight into the hills,
the coyotes, you'll hear them barking far off,
you know they can see you driving in.
By now Mt. Lassen might have snow,
the streams could be full and running, the air so crisp,
the leaves of aspens, color of earth and wheat.
There is a place there that has heard no human voice,
no words, just the quick suck of air,
tongues running over teeth.

The End of Time

She lived just up
the long dirt road.
It was no secret
that her parents
were alcoholics.
They told me her father
shot her mother,
then himself.
One bullet into the roof
of his mouth.
We were thirteen
when she went to stay
with the Maxwells.
We stopped playing
those silly games
of monk and chimp.
We stopped writing
to each other.
Later, I heard
she was married,
her two year old daughter
dying of leukemia.
I can still see us,
skipping past
the old abandoned house
on Bear Creek Road
singing that song
we made up
about the end of time.

McCloud 1952

The old wooden sidewalk
clattered and creaked
under our feet.
We hurried past the steam vents
remembering the stories
of black widow spiders.
We didn't know his name,
but everyday
he would step off
the sidewalk,
hat in hand
to let us pass.
He was old and black,
a janitor at the mill.

I don't remember
if we planned it.
One day we jumped to the side
before he could get off,
smiled and said,
Good morning.
First surprise,
then a look of fear and pain
crossed his face.
We stumbled awkwardly.
He walked away.
We felt sick inside,
ashamed.

That evening, I walked down
to the creek to skip stones
the water was so still,
like it had been that way
for a hundred years.
I know that to open to someone
is to pull an unknown history
right into you,
then to live with it
growing in you;
until what you remember
his black face,
the way your own face
stared back at you
from the water.

Mt. Shasta

Last night I dreamed
it was a bedroom window
white curtain drawn
window slightly lifted.
The shadow of a big pine
ominously whining & waving
in the wind.
You could hear breathing there
under the heavy dark quilt.
Someone moving in the next room
like a sleepwalker.

Looking out the window,
you would be gazing north
toward the mountain.
Everything terrible
came from the mountain.
Everything tender.
Everything you could not speak
was sent there,
from there returned,
disguised as snow
or moonlight.

The Bears on Firebreak Road

On those long summer evenings,
we'd drive out the firebreak road.
Sun slowly going down,
forest burned black,
no moon.
The high pitched cry
of a mountain lion
sounding down the hill.

We'd turn out the lights. Wait.
Eyes strained
toward the edge of the woods,
where it slanted
away from the creek
until they came,
heavy in their bodies
black as night.

Our bodies
like theirs
lumbered heavily
against each other.

Returning to Bear Creek

She says *desire.*
Something unaltered
pulling inside her.
Here the thing is nameless.
Here the minnows
brush her legs
like his tongue
that first time.

She follows the sinuous bend
of the creek. Stops,
where it curves along the bank.
She dreams the dry riverbed:
many colored river stones
color of silt
willow branches.
She dreams her body
like the river throbs
in its hurrying.

She says *love*
the dark smell of sex.
She says *desire.*

In Memory of My Father

The desert, he said,
belongs to the creatures.
He knew them well,
caught rattlers with a stick
gave me the dried empty tails.
I stacked them together.
I remember the largest,
nine rattles.
He was a big man.
Sometimes he held my face
in his large dark hands
whispering, *Sweet girl,*
sweet darlin'.
At times a shadow
would come across him,
not even my mother's voice
could bring him back.
He had a stroke when I was fifteen,
it was hard to move him.
He was a big man,
my mother was small,
four feet ten,
I was fifteen.
We moved him carefully,
the way I moved those tails,
room to room
year to year.

It was a long time before I could tell anyone
the way I'm telling you now.
Once, when he lay still but awake,
I quietly entered the room,
to get a sweater from the drawer.
With his right hand
he grabbed me,
held me there,
tears streaming down his face.
Just now I had to walk outside
to see for myself
that the stars were as clear
as I had remembered them.
He held me there
as though there were some truth
we must share
some truth he could not speak.
If I could open that door,
I could see
the long red cloth
over the bureau.
The Indian ring,
my mother keeps
behind glass.
The way he held my face,
in those large stained hands,
whispering,
Sweet girl,
sweet darlin'.

Visiting My Father's Grave

Sometimes it isn't comfort we're after.
It isn't even warmth.
It's how to say snow
in its deepest parts.
It's how to say Bear Creek
meaning the dark blue current
hitting underwater boulders
of the deepest gray
grainy like sand.
It's how to say
the red pearl color of dusk,
or rain
lashing around his grave.

Jung calls the *five* in the dream the number
of the natural man / woman, by which he means
one who is in touch with his / her spiritual instincts.

Buffalo Five, I

It was one of those five line poems.
The title was *Buffalo Five.*
It was a good poem,
then I woke up,
trying to remember
the last two lines.
Some sort of message.
I thought I wrote it down,
now I struggle along knowing
that somebody's poem is lost.
I have the title,
Buffalo Five, five lines.
The message was old.
It was a song heard deep,
moving across the plains.
I know that to get that message
I would have to go on sleeping
or take mushrooms
or sweat in that house
that keeps collapsing,
the one that heard
Melvin Chiloquin murmur:
Pitiful, just pitiful.

Buffalo Five, II

Maybe it was a long path
leading to the house
lined with wild roses.
They were pink roses.
Inside there was a lamp,
the shade: stretched deerskin
the stand: legs of a deer.
I ran my fingers down the stiff
hairy legs, over the smooth hooves,
dreaming animals alive,
quick in the fields.

There was a small jar of gold nuggets.
I spilled them upon the table
dreaming sunlight on the water.
Maybe it was a garden of rocks
cinder rock, lava rock.
Maybe there were red and yellow tulips,
a whole bed of them.
Maybe there was a man
who sat outside the shed
on some old stairs,
staring into a mining pan.

Not for as far as you can see:
Buffalo.

Buffalo Five, III

It was one dusty mile
from the rock garden
to Bear Creek.
Beneath the trestle
on the south side of the creek
cattle grazed.
They were not buffalo.
They had not come out of the dust.
They did not carry
their own deaths with them.

Sometimes
just after waking
we would see them
in the dim lit dawn
looking up,
as though
remembering something.
The tall yellow grass
moved
just slightly.

Dedication Poem

Running   passing waters
she enters the wilderness
and silently is thrust
upon the universe.

Running   holding wildness
in her hand
she sighs
upon this land
she heaves and sighs
upon this land.

Tie up your scarf tonight
these boy are out for
blood tonight ~ Lumineers

Walking Toward Ten Mile River

I walk toward Ten Mile River.
The hills above Elk
are covered with flowers.
The Elk beach where the Greenwood creek
runs in three channels to the sea.
Red tail hawk, steelhead, raven.
I walk along a path lined
with the bushes of small birds.
I make camp on the beach.
It is a good beginning.
They say Ten Mile River
is close to the beach.
I lay facing south
on a brilliant noon day.
I am from the
Manchester Pomo band,
gathering ceanothus
and the bark from coffeeberry trees.
I gather shells
walk north up the beach.
The air grows cold,
a swarm of mountains appear
between me and Ten Mile River.
Moonlight whispers over trees
stones, charred mammal bones.
I stop to listen for secrets in the grass.
Night raises itself over the last hills.

Tiger Lilies

Today, I pruned
the flowering quince
& the Japanese maple.
Once, I came upon
a field of wild tiger lilies
hundreds of them
some three,
four feet high
living in a wet marsh
high in the mountains.

A field of wild tiger lilies,
flowering quince,
Japanese maple,
& Oregon Juncoes.
Never mind
which is past
or present.
It's how they
offer themselves
without edges
singing.

There Shall be a Legend

There shall be a legend
made of these times,

you shall be its chief.

The road will spiral
towards myths that shine
in light of an arrow
pointed toward the east.

In this legend
lie both bird and beast.

And they shall spread
over the earth like stones
sand will scatter with the four winds
old age will walk beside them.

Water will flow from their roots.

And you shall master the stars with songs
walk to the beating of wings
run to the roaring water in the canyon.

There shall be a legend
made of these times,

you shall be its chief.

In this legend
lie both bird and beast.

For Eva, Upon Turning Fifteen

It isn't my life Eve,
it isn't even yours,
until one day
you find yourself
looking back,
by then you're looking up.
Aaron was saying
how it was
when he was a kid,
being so close to the earth,
how you oriented that way.
The smells,
like the leather of old army boots,
how that reminded him of Inverness,
or the grass
the eucalyptus.
Then Sam said how as a kid
he couldn't get close enough to it.
He would lay down on it
with his eye right to the ground.
Then you find yourself
grown up
more and more you look up
away from the earth.

It isn't my life Eve,
I want to tell you.
It's more how your life
tells me.
How we remind each other of something.
How your choices make themselves
drive deeper,
almost like they might fall
out of this world,
akin to a past
more than mine.
It's like desire,
how your body is drawn to it,
a stitch at a time,
how passion becomes the real work.

It isn't my life Eve.
It's the way
everything repeats itself.
How the seasons,
like the way we stopped
and counted the daffodils again,
or the way the dusk
settled
archaic
bit by bit.

Name Origin Poem

One night I walked
deep into the woods
You'd have thought I left,
but really I was more
coming than going.

The woods opened up
with these sucking noises.
Then crow flew by
between two trees
soaring on his side.

I began to grow moss for hair.
Something in me was always coming out,
climbing or going down
close to the fire
sitting up all night.

I was always there
for the casting of shadows
the ones that know the black ends of night.
While walking I found many dark things.
The moist earth was my fragrance.

I did nothing.
I sat alone for whole days.
I listened for my country, any country.
I slept at night surrounded by Yucca.
The stark guards of dreams.

I pulled old songs and memories
around me like a blanket.
I drank only from stones.
Later,
I became Kiva.

The Dark Burdens Flew Up

The storm approached
from the south.
A sudden blast of wind.
Dreams broke apart.
Life lost its boundaries.
The interior had been loosened.
The dark burdens flew up
into the hills behind Elk.

Another sudden wind.
Silence broke into song.
Cypress gave way
while the old bark
of redwoods
dark, unforgiving
covered the earth.
The radiant wind
moved along the still banks
of stars.

A Tribute to Afternoon

I came home from work. It was 5 o'clock. The color
the afternoon light cast on the man-with-tongue sculpture
in the garden was mauve. I wanted to place a rose in his
hand. I wanted to pick strawberries and lay them upon
his tongue and whisper how all the afternoons slip by
unwitnessed. He knows the secrets of many afternoons.
He lies with violet columbine, plum and lavender.
Now the light fades and all around is green. The sky
grows pale and giant redwoods hold the last light.

Each day I am away, I dream the road that winds
through the oak forest, the years it has taken
McDonald's grapevines to spread out and grow up the
500 year old redwood stumps. There is one afternoon
that catches the brilliant pink blooms of the cactus.
The first bloom burst forth in such glory, I hid from it.
In its hunger for a melody I could not give, it died.

I dream the guards of afternoon, witness time stretching
across the dry fields of summer. In the center of the field
straw piled in bundles, wired shut,

then exploding, carefully drifting back into place.
The meadow is bathed in the memory of other
afternoons. I began to lust for them, for the low hills
which lie open, vulnerable as a woman in love, as a
mother is to her son.

In this one afternoon desire ran rampant as the
mountain streams of my youth. I vowed to my ancestors
to love the earth back into living, to feed the afternoons
from my own mouth, to use my last breath to blow
wind through the dry grass. Afternoons of the past
crowd around me, demanding to know where I've been.
I whisper how I've been locked away so long,
I shattered like glass. They share with me a true story.
I cut one lock of my hair and give them: memory.

Today the Wind Makes Sounds No One's Heard Before

for Essie Parrish

Walking the Mendocino Headlands
we stop to see the place
where they dug up the body.
The strong wind
hoisting waves up
onto the shore.
Rolling water crashing
into that place.
We tried to look in there
where the grave must have been.
Wind blew dirt in our eyes,
all the elements urging us
away from there.

Walking back home,
wind raging at our backs,
moon full in the east,
sun setting in the west.
Sam said, *The sun and the moon*
are having a conversation,
that's what this wind is about.

I remember another grave,
no coffin,
the body wrapped
maybe in some cloth or skin,
a mound of earth covering it.

Today the wind makes sounds
no one's heard before.
It says each grave
was meant to be final.
It says the dead do not forget
the place where they left the body.
It says when you open something
things come toward you.

God Speaks

Minstrel of Wrath

Even as we walk by that place
where the grave had been
some 80 - 90 years.

Even when the wind
forced us away from there.

Even as we lie together now,
close as a single body.

Still the sea rages there
and that wind:
a minstrel of wrath.

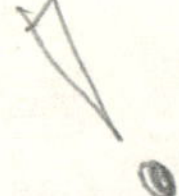

The Last of the Dreamers

for Essie Parish

I read recently 30,000 wild geese landed
somewhere around a pond
in the Delta.
This morning,
I counted fourteen quail scurrying
across the road.
In the redwoods
a dove landed on a top branch
swaying in the wind,
wings heavy with rain.

Last night I dreamed my shoulder drooped
like a wounded wing.
I began to look for some pattern of connection,
something that would cradle this mouth full of longing.
For what? The old migration of birds?
The dust of a red earth?
A gathering of crows at the trail head?
For a language that is both guttural and grieving?
Then I saw her, shaking her long braids like a prayer.
She said: *I am the last of the dreamers.*

Now I understand,
that the injured wing was a recognition,
some sort of code the body knows.
While this is a time of terrible loneliness,
it is also a time of preparation,
a time to listen carefully to the wind and the sea.
A time to understand that we are still of this earth,
and that to raise the veil
is to welcome back the old ones, the dreamers,
is to acknowledge our beloved home,
is to stand in the light and be counted.

This is an Indian Wind,
1000 Business Cards are Blowing Down the Red Road

Tonight on the Mendocino Headlands,
we catch sight of the gray whales
heading south.
The sky drawn back.
A tumult of yellow grass waving.
The light seeming on the edge of the world.
I think of what awaits them,
what awaits us.

I think of the oil rigs,
of the oil soaked birds
we carried from the beach
on Limantour Spit,
so many years ago.
If language could move stones,
we might hear the heartbeat,
of what lies beneath this arid earth.

The wind speaks.
We burn.
We live with such indignation.
Take it into the body
sleep with it,
this keen wound.

Dream in denial
that this emptiness is temporary.

Tonight the wind releases memory.
Buffalo graze on the bluffs.
This is all wrong,
I know that.
In a dream,
there is an Indian Wind,
1000 business cards
are blowing down the red road.

The Rain

Eva writes from Porte Viejo,
Reggae plays everywhere, day & night.
Church services are held,
where they sing like crazy.
I hang out, even in the rain to listen.

The rain comes down.
Long slow tears of the hungry.
Feather wet tears of grief.
Women carry their babies, heads dangling;
two hearts ticking over blood blue bones.

Rain all day becomes blue evening.
A woman's son is dying.
She carries him within her body
bearing & releasing him like birth,
like dying inside a radiant light.

Rainwater. Seedbirth.
Breath like silk over his psychic bones.
Sing like crazy.
Sing the long slow tears of the hungry.
Sing the feather wet tears of grief.

Rain all night, blue morning.
Breath like silk over their psychic bones.
Sing like crazy.
Sing the long slow tears of the hungry.
Sing the feather wet tears of grief.

Since That Moment in Elk

Since that moment in Elk
when the storm came,
gale winds foretold,
the obliteration of memory;
I have been silent in the night,
receiving
the impenetrable darkness
of my inner country
deep into myself.

Since that moment in Elk,
when the ridge lay covered
with unforgiving branches of redwood
I have been quiet in my heart
receiving
the heavy cloth
uniting bodies with the earth.

Since that moment in Elk,
when ancestral figures
moved down the wide rivers
chanting their grave songs;
I have mourned the dead
in Khaji, in Basra &
the scorched earth of Baghdad.

Tonight, and perhaps for always:

The many men who would soldier their countries
are pacing inside me.

The women   I hold   like sunlight in my eyes.

The children
tiny figures of grief
I fasten in my hair
with combs and beads.

Their Tears Like Songs

Their voices reach me
even at this great distance
warn me to keep looking
into the deep mystery
that is my life.

They spoke to me in that dream
where the inner body twisting
out of its skin rose up,
birdlike, skeletal and tender.

They told me that my voice was chosen
that the silence I have known all my life
would be broken
that songs would pour forth like tears.

Every morning, I rise before dawn
faint chanting voices like tiny bells
pierce the dark ice of my heart.

If I could sing, it would sound like a swift wind
carried along riverbanks
it would sound like buffalo stampeding over plains
it would sound furious and beating like wings
it would sound like the grief of children
in Bosnia, in Rwanda
their tears like songs taken up by angels.

Roses at Dusk

Grief made me come here
dragging an old wicker chair
into the dim light.
It is late, late afternoon
almost early evening.
The body waits,
remembers a sudden shift
in the wind at 4 o'clock.
The precise moment
red poppies begin to close.
Oak shadows move
along the eaves of the bathhouse.
In this mauve light,
Sam's carvings
turn a deep russet-brown.

Grief made me come here.
Like an unseen wave
it colors everything blue.
Woods deepen behind me.
Eerie, unapproachable shadows
fill me with fear and loneliness.
I cannot keep from staring
into that place.
Roots of memory

sprawled
in that dark.
There is no way to know
how close we are to each other,
how in tune,
how perfectly harmonized.
Our friendship:
roses at dusk.
The inner heart
beats across the miles
between us.
In a latihan dream,
I felt you moving
like silk,
above the burning earth.
Translucent unhurried
yet certain of the course.

Grief made me come here.
Seated on an old wicker chair
speaking in a voice
that struggles to recognize itself.
Something rises up
more alone now,
more alive.
Something about this moment
this secret light
this dazzling silence.

Ancient Grace

The way I looked at you recently,
do you remember?
I had just given you a card.
The picture was of an old Indian woman
looking back,
and a young dark haired Indian girl
looking forward.

Together we sat
on a stump
in an unknown place.
Maybe we had been there before
or maybe we had just arrived.

We were both quiet,
respectful of who we are
and where we are going,
knowing that our inner song is safe,
always with each other and with God.

That night I dreamed
we were riding horses,
far back into the woods
behind the house.

We rode late,
camped by the river.
When you called me,
I heard your voice
traveling over time.

Like an ancient grace
it descended down below,
up above,
all around us.

Something Buried Deep Turns Over

Rain after the equinox.
The wet & darkened earth
burning in my breasts.

Something buried deep
turns over
rises   subsides   rises.

Then grows quiet
in the dark deepening body
of the rain.

How the Artist Dreams

Tonight I am so close,
so close to something.
I cannot define for you.
It has to do with the child,
with ponies & the age of your parents,
with all the dead grass of winter,
the dense fog across the road,
old age that walks straight forward,
the same as day passes to night.
It has to do with the death of children,
about looking into the eyes of the innocent,
the struggle to get back on your feet
after a few good blows,
the way the winter orchards stand
stark in the fields in March,
the way mornings flock together,
how the artist dreams,
the picture forming way back.

I Created the Morning for You

I created the morning for you.
These children
made from blood and wet tears
are yours.
The war you fought?
I didn't know about that.
I only knew that I was tired
waiting to die
so I gave birth
three times writhing
then pushing carriages
up Third Avenue hill
pushing them
to cross the streets
knowing that these
are the same children
everywhere.

I wheeled them into playgrounds
lined them up myself
that I did not see
the rows of empty boots.
I sang lullabies
every time I heard you scream.
I stood up
while you crouched.

I threw my head back laughing
while your eyes sank into your head
weighted with sadness.
Every time I tried to be a woman
I stumbled into holes
and was thrown out again.
Memories rise
from dead ashes
I buried in the basement
from the photographs of burning nuns.
I was always running in the streets.
In 1945 a man ran shouting,
Roosevelt is dead,
get off the streets.

RUN GIRL RUN.
Run like lemmings
down a one way street.

Still, I created the morning for you
it crawled out of a warm spot
on my hand and kept spilling out
over your dreams, until
awake, I heard you scream,
and then: lay me down to sleep.
I took up marching then

marching in the streets
babies on my back
slung over my hips
with my head thrown back laughing.
No one dies marching.

Phosphorescent flares
occasional fire crackers
of goodwill.
Strong bodies in line
marching against the war.
Shadows of men
propped up between wires.

Worlds apart
each in his,
her own hell.

RUN GIRL RUN.

Still, I created the morning for you.

The Light

for Charles Simon Steinbuck

The light has gone out
of his body.
The light.
The sun will never shine
on his body.
The sun.
The body.
The light.
His body will never shine
on the sun.
The body.
The light.
Gone out.
The light gone.
Out of his body.
The sun shines
on the light gone
out of his body.

What Lays Waste

Having said a part
of what runs through these veins.

Having told
of one river's theme
I cannot tell more   now.

What weighs on my heart
lays waste   lays waste
my art.

Baskets Overflowing

Let me come along
On this road you travel
Without knowing where we go
How shall we know each other
Except by these authentic memories?

Let us say it then
Let us follow the compass through cornfields
Until we come out on the other side
Bare   transparent
Speaking the old language.

Siksika   Etzikorn   Nitsinixki
Until we gather all the unspoken words
Until light splinters the dark
Until the years begin to flow backwards
& we arrive home

our baskets overflowing.

Lily Full of Grace

Lily's skin was white
Her name chosen
It had the sound of small birds
Like quail running fast
The solstice has just passed
Trees darken the hillside
White sheep outline the meadow

When Eliza came to visit
I wanted to say an invocation
I wanted to bless our time together
I wanted to go back
Oh let's go back holding hands
We could even skip over the bitterness
We could be young again
We could be childless
Were we ever childless together?
Were they always there, the children?
Were they our everlasting,
Our unbearable loveliness,
Our little fierce birds,
Our solitary longing for ourselves?

Out of kindness Eliza took a photo
Of the tree I planted for Lily

Wait, the sun has gone down on this barrenness
Wait the leaves have fallen
Oh not this shadow
Not this limp Japanese maple
Not this pitiful gesture
Ending in some photograph

It began with our embrace   our tears
It began in the soft light of evening
When we both knew
No one else would be coming through the door
Not this night   not ever
The thought could drive you mad
Or you could   as we did
Lengthen our gaze
Shift toward the darkness
Let it all enter
Like some huge blue wall
Until finally standing together
We arrived at that place
We carried her home
Her frailness like the tree wavered
Together we arrived here
Where only birds pass through
She was that light
Where burial wrappings are loosened
And her loveliness enters
Where mercy shows itself
In this moment
Lily   full of grace.

Nikaomatsipiiyohsi

I called my spirit to join me as I travel

When my oldest sister called
she sang me a nursery rhyme
our father sang to her over 84 years ago.
She spelled it out phonetically
as the language was only his.
It began: *Top Gay Bunny*
Top Gay Bunny
Top Cee Zee Saun SetSinnyhop
ThraPeeZee ISaw

As she sang in her two-year-old voice
I was lifted right out of my body
I seemed to be flying back in time.

There must have been that moment
in the woods when everything was still
when he may have whispered
or maybe it was a gesture I could understand
or a song he sang or the way his profile
spoke to me   somewhere way back then
I always knew he was an Indian man
with a secret I was to carry all my life.

Thinking back, I felt honored then as I do now
to remember the ways he taught me in the woods
to remember how gentle he was, how his strength
made me feel safe. I felt him through his childhood of grief,
I feel him through mine, I feel him through my children,
and now my grandchildren.
I hear him say the Blackfoot words for buffalo: *iinii*
for wolf: *omahkapiísi*, for bobcat: *natayo.*

In my memory, in my words,

thus I honor him.

Deliverance

for Haiti, January 10, 2010

Does the name define the body?
the soul?
Who is the *I* then?
When the little one cries out,
Mama, please do not let me die.
We hear the words as though they are ours,
we are the ones buried there,
not those bright calm eyes looking back.

Didn't this already happen?
Wasn't Katrina enough?
Was she her name?
Was the cement solid?
Was her terror ours?
Is the *I* dissolving?
Are we all victims of a fate
that cannot be changed?

Not by a name
Not by choosing a different path
Not by all the victims calling out at once
Nothing can change the babies who live
From those who die.

Was this necessary?
If you tell me it was,
I will not believe you.
I will call you a false prophet.
I will say to abandon hope is to change reality.
If you saw her belief,
her tremendous courage,
the endearing braids crusted with dust.
you would say, *I am changed.*
You would say that this great upheaval,
this loss, is life as it presents itself.

And that the child, all the children who suffer
are one heart exposed.
We cannot be spared their suffering,
we can only concentrate,
we can only labor,
we can only cry out with them,
Have mercy,
until it is over.

It is in this
exceptional moment
of notice,
of witness,
that we are surrendered,
delivered by those souls
transforming
creation itself.

Something Else

for Haiti, January 10, 2010

They came out singing
They crawled out from their concrete graves
Praising God
As they lay in their makeshift cots
Their eyes sang to us
Comforted us
Gave thanks to us
Their arms reaching up above their heads
Triumphant as any sunrise.

Something else was moving there
Besides the earth
Something released   given back
Darkness hauling into light
Death needs a witness
Something else under the concrete
Lives in us now
Sings their faith
We are not afraid

Their voices rising up into a luminous
honey-filled light.

Tucson, Arizona

for Gabrielle Giffords
January 8, 2011

I

I might write about the specific event
But the aching for the fallen
And the one who felled them
Would be the same
Even the victims would say:
You are not to blame.
No words can halt what happened.

I imagine a whole nation in grief
Nothing can make it stop
I imagine a room full of flowers
A field of innocent white lambs
I imagine some winged bird
Who would swoop down
Across this field of impossibilities.

Who would see with eagle eyes
How they were all carried away
Disappeared
Silenced
I imagine far off   so far off
The dead weeping for us
For what we must endure.

II

Always in moments like these
I go back to that football field
where we lay tangled in deep summer grass
My lavender dress
spread out in shantung glory
Our lips lingering
the sky so wide
forming the roof of our world.

In moments like these
when the events of men
break open a wounded heart
I go back to that tenderness
that unattainable longing
to name things simply:
River Tree Rock.

I would crawl on hands and knees
to find the light in all of this
To hear the cadence of what
was once called grace.

"Rasunah Katz's poems read like a poetic mantra that memorializes and celebrates *spirit of place* with a power and clarity that is staggering. The gift of these poems is that they allow the reader to go on a visionary journey. The poems chart a landscape of myth, dream, memory, life or death, and ultimately are poems of transcendence for the human spirit. With great poignancy and compassion, these poems enliven our spirits with that magical essence that is much larger than our individual lives. *I know that to open to someone / is to pull an unknown history / right into you. / then live with it / growing in you;* The gift of the poems in *Buffalo Five* is that they are inclusive of spirit, nature and family and ultimately transport us to that primal mystery of what it means to be human."
-Devreaux Baker,
author of *Red Willow People* and *Beyond the Circumstance of Sight*

"In the middle of the night the other thoughts come out, the ones we don't share for fear of driving our friends away for fear that, spoken aloud, they may prove to be more real than the perceptions of the day. Rasunah's poems provide a sanctuary, a candle to light those thoughts and perceptions, permitting us to observe them with a sense of detachment and, ultimately, to witness our own lives whole—validating our despair as well as our joy. She does this with a sensuous use of language whose sound reminds us that poetry is at root an oral rather than a literate art."
-CJ Cassidy

"*I began to lust of them, for the low hills / which lie open, vulnerable as a woman in love, as a / mother is to her son.* It has been my great luck and privilege to know Rasunah's poems through the whole of my own life birthing poems. She has enhanced, empowered, instructed me. Mystical, bonded with the land, family, the human body, psyche and soul, her poems pierce the veil of time and place. *It's an opening so deep / that all the ancestors enter / then you're tied forever.* Rasunah Katz's *Buffalo Five* is a new integration of spiritual and instinctual energy emerging."
-Sharon Doubiago,
author of *Hard Country; South America Mi Hija;* and *My Father's Love*

"I like them very much for the poetry contained in them. Some of the lines and images are so luscious and distinctive. The names were all there, Pondosa, the small logging camp between McCloud and Burney Falls, Bear Creek, the mountain. That kind of writing is so clear."
-Simon Ortiz, author of *Sand Creek* and *Woven Stone*

About the Author

Rasunah Katz has made her home in Elk, California on the Mendocino Coast since 1972. A Pushcart Prize nominee, she has published poems in anthologies, literary journals and magazines. *Buffalo Five* is her first collection.